Audio Access Included

PIANO SOLO

OPERA
WITH A
TOUCH OF JAZZ

18 BELOVED MASTERPIECES
ARRANGED BY
LEE EVANS

T0056603

To access audio, visit:
www.halleonard.com/mylibrary

Enter Code
5199-6543-6001-7932

ISBN 978-1-4950-8278-8

HAL•LEONARD®
7777 W. BLUEMOUND RD. P.O. BOX 13819 MILWAUKEE, WI 53213

Visit Hal Leonard Online at
www.halleonard.com

PREFACE

For me, the primary appeal of opera—staged sung music and drama which had its beginnings in the 16th and 17th centuries—has always resided more in the musical, rather than the dramatic, content. To opera purists, this may sound like heresy of a sort, but thus has it always been for me. In my teenage years, when I first began attending live opera and ballet performances in my hometown of New York City, I remember often closing my eyes so that I would not be distracted by the action taking place on stage, and could focus on the music.

This book is a sequel to *Classics with a Touch of Jazz* in which, similarly, I add jazz stylings to masterpieces of classical music, consistent with my decades-long mission to incorporate jazz concepts into classical music pedagogy as a motivational tool for piano students and teachers alike.

Note that one piece in the collection—Richard Wagner's "Siegfried Idyll"—was a symphonic poem that Wagner presented as a gift to his wife to celebrate the birth of their son, Siegfried. I'm including it in this collection because Wagner was primarily an opera composer, and because the work is simply gorgeous. In fact, he incorporated some of its themes into the opera *Siegfried*.

It is my fervent hope that this volume (complete with audio recordings online) will provide many hours of pure enjoyment, and perhaps introduce the representative great literature of this marvelous genre to a new generation.

Lee Evans

CONTENTS

CILEA

49 Il lamento di Federico
L'ARLESIANA

DONIZETTI

34 Chi raffrena il mio furore
LUCIA DI LAMMERMOOR

39 Una furtiva lagrima
L'ELISIR D'AMORE

GLUCK

12 Dance of the Blessed Spirits
ORFEO ED EURIDICE

MASCAGNI

22 Intermezzo
CAVALLERIA RUSTICANA

MASSENET

24 Meditation
THAÏS

PUCCINI

8 Che gelida manina
LA BOHÈME

4 E lucevan le stelle
TOSCA

20 Mi chiamano Mimì
LA BOHÈME

36 O mio babbino caro
GIANNI SCHICCHI

44 Quando me'n vo'
LA BOHÈME

17 Vissi d'arte
TOSCA

PURCELL

28 When I Am Laid in Earth
DIDO AND AENEAS

SAINT-SAËNS

31 Mon cœur s'ouvre à ta voix
SAMSON ET DELILAH

TCHAIKOVSKY

42 Lensky's Aria
EUGENE ONEGIN

WAGNER

52 Siegfried Idyll

46 Walther's Prize Song
DIE MEISTERSINGER

VERDI

14 Addio, del passato
LA TRAVIATA

E LUCEVAN LE STELLE
(And the stars were brightly shining)
from TOSCA

GIACOMO PUCCINI
Arranged by LEE EVANS

Very slowly ♩ = 72

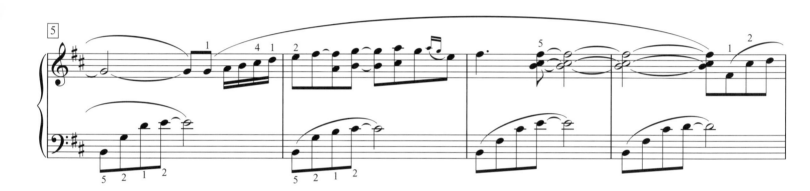

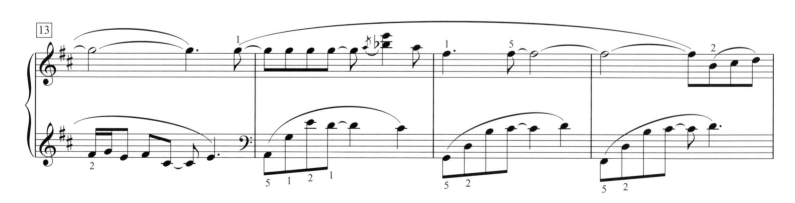

CHE GELIDA MANINA
(What a frozen little hand)
from LA BOHÈME

GIACOMO PUCCINI
Arranged by LEE EVANS

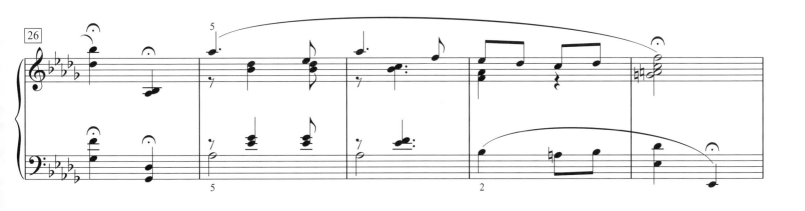

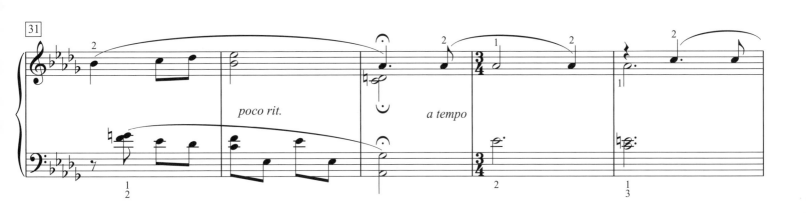

DANCE OF THE BLESSED SPIRITS
from ORFEO ED EURIDICE

CHRISTOPH WILLIBALD GLUCK
Arranged by LEE EVANS

ADDIO, DEL PASSATO
(Farewell, happy dreams of the past)
from LA TRAVIATA

GIUSEPPE VERDI
Arranged by LEE EVANS

VISSI D'ARTE
(I lived for art)
from TOSCA

GIACOMO PUCCINI
Arranged by LEE EVANS

MI CHIAMANO MIMÌ
(They call me Mimi)
from LA BOHÈME

GIACOMO PUCCINI
Arranged by LEE EVANS

21

INTERMEZZO
from CAVALLERIA RUSTICANA

PIETRO MASCAGNI
Arranged by LEE EVANS

MEDITATION
from THAÏS

JULES MASSENET
Arranged by LEE EVANS

WHEN I AM LAID IN EARTH
from DIDO AND AENEAS

HENRY PURCELL
Arranged by LEE EVANS

MON CŒUR S'OUVRE À TA VOIX

(My heart opens to your voice)

from SAMSON AND DELILAH

CAMILLE SAINT-SAËNS
Arranged by LEE EVANS

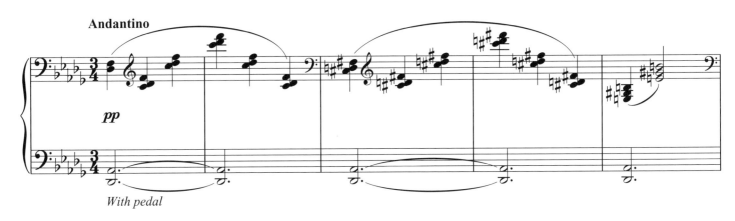

CHI RAFFRENA IL MIO FURORE
(Who restrains my fury)
Sextet from LUCIA DI LAMMERMOOR

GAETANO DONIZETTI
Arranged by LEE EVANS

O MIO BABBINO CARO
(O my beloved daddy)
from GIANNI SCHICCHI

GIACOMO PUCCINI
Arranged by LEE EVANS

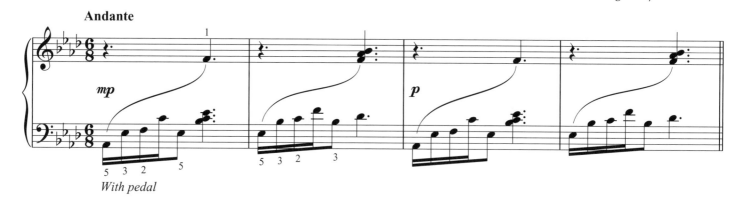

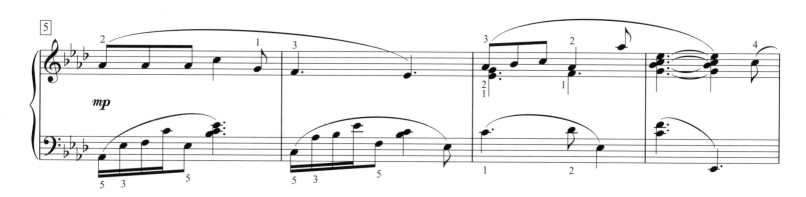

UNA FURTIVA LAGRIMA
(A secret tear)
from L'ELISIR D'AMORE

GAETANO DONIZETTI
Arranged by LEE EVANS

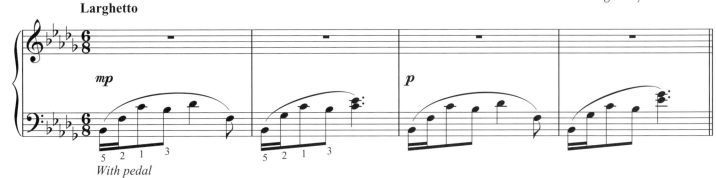

Larghetto

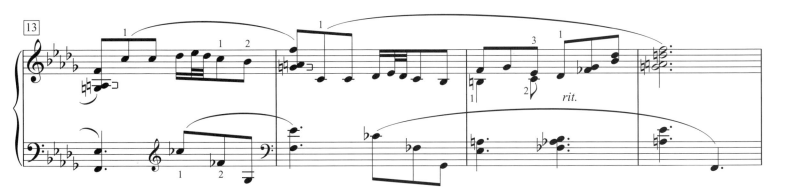

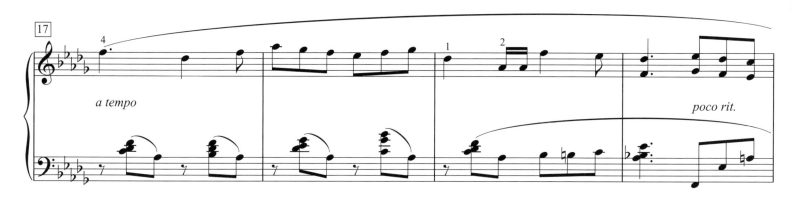

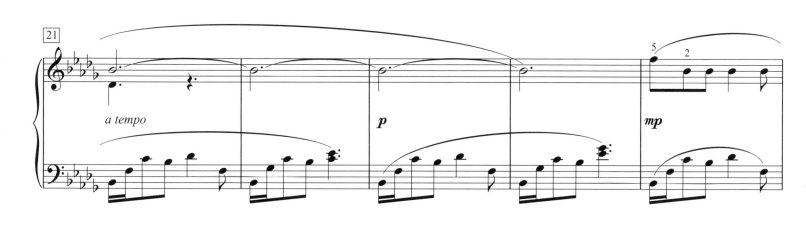

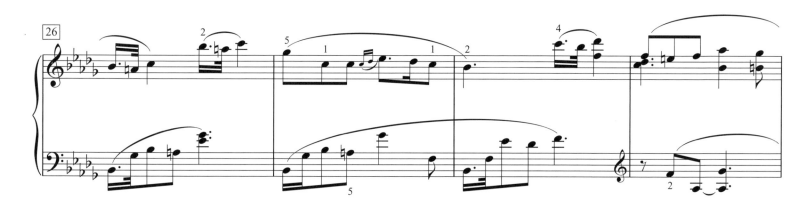

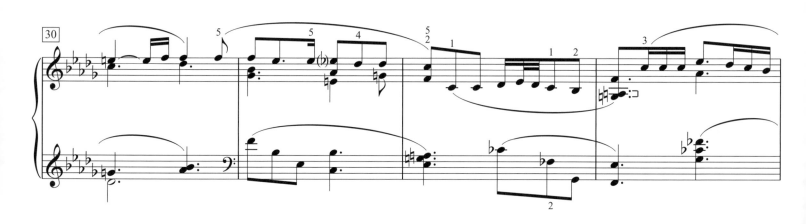

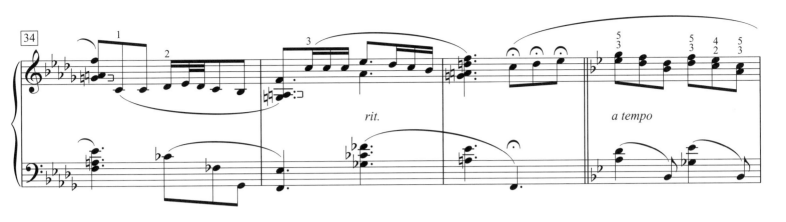

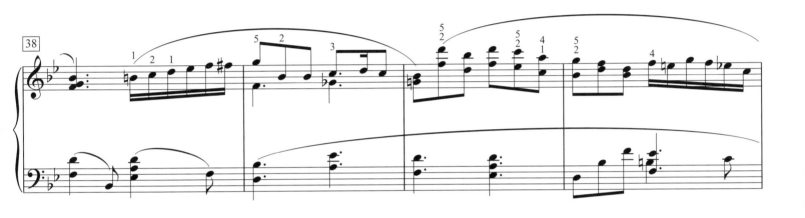

LENSKY'S ARIA
from EUGENE ONEGIN

PYOTR IL'YICH TCHAIKOVSKY
Arranged by LEE EVANS

Andante; rubato

QUANDO ME'N VO'
(When I go out)
from LA BOHÈME

GIACOMO PUCCINI
Arranged by LEE EVANS

WALTHER'S PRIZE SONG
from DIE MEISTERSINGER

RICHARD WAGNER
Arranged by LEE EVANS

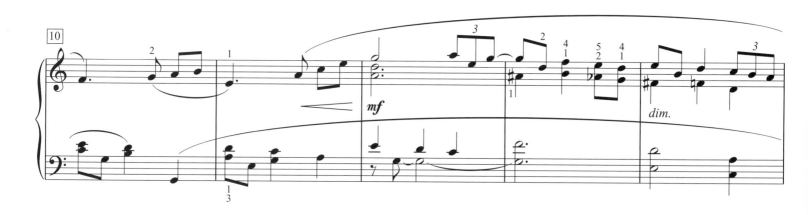

IL LAMENTO DI FEDERICO
(Federico's Lament)
from L'ARLESIANA

FRANCESCO CILEA
Arranged by LEE EVANS

Molto sostenuto ♩ = 60

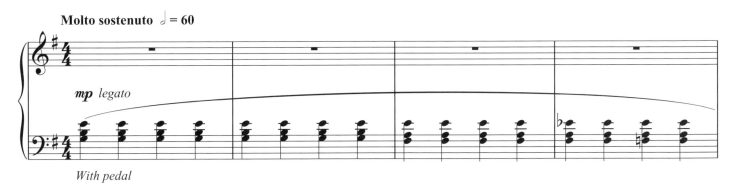

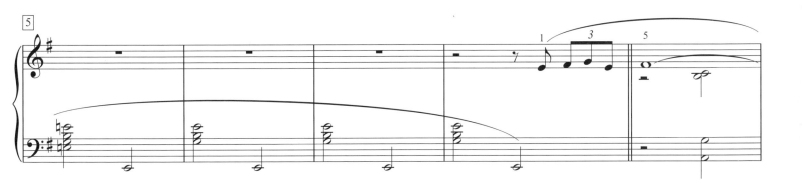

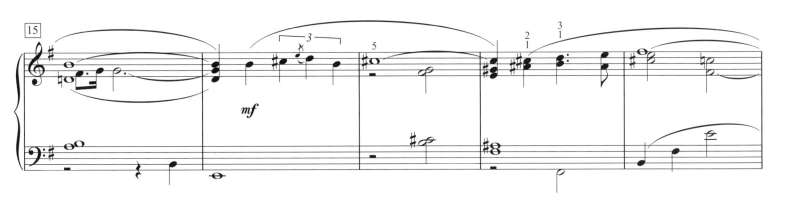

SIEGFRIED IDYLL

RICHARD WAGNER
Arranged by LEE EVANS

Quietly and slowly

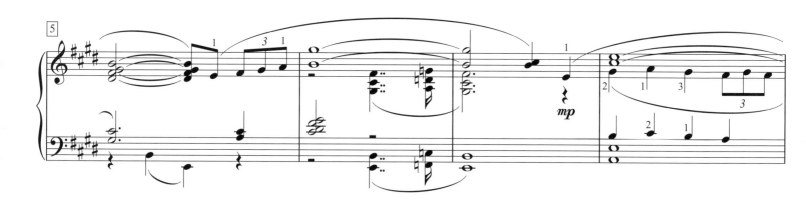

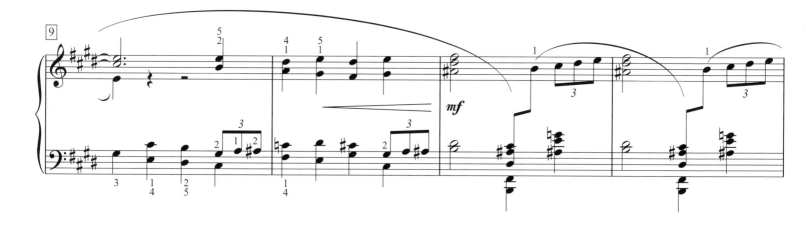

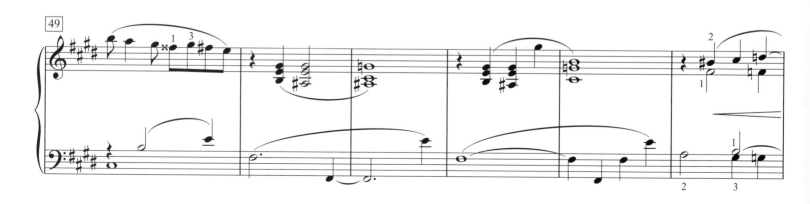

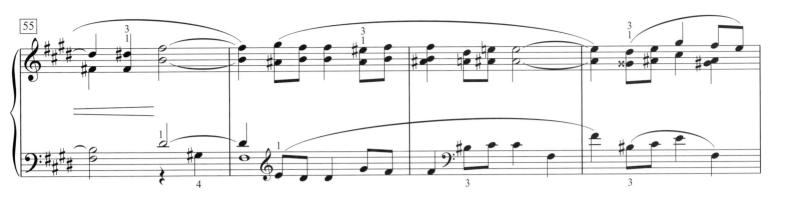

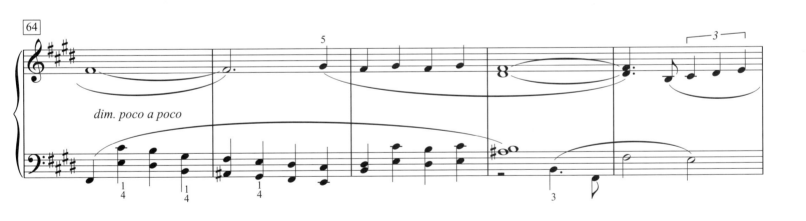

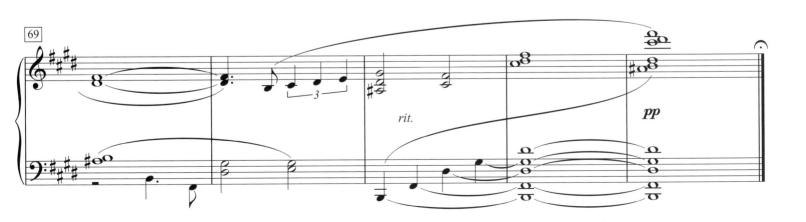

ALSO BY

LEE EVANS

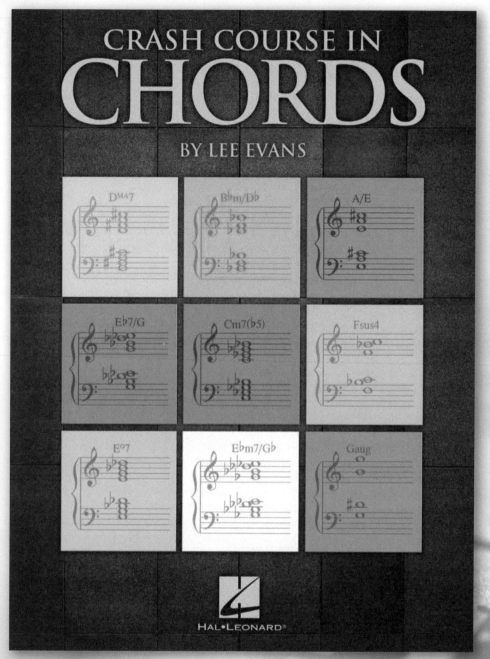

HL00296864

An indispensable theory and performance workbook packed with everything the intermediate-level student needs to know about chords. Pianists and non-pianists alike will benefit from the written exercises covering everything from basic triads and 7th chords to inversions, transposition, harmonization and more. Lee Evans explains concepts in easy-to-understand language and immediately applies them in a variety of performance exercises and lead sheet examples. A must for every music student!